# GARAGE GIRLS

CANDACE MILES, MADELAINE NUNN
and ANNA RODWAY

**CURRENCY PRESS**
The performing arts publisher

CURRENT THEATRE SERIES

First published in 2024
by Currency Press Pty Ltd,
Gadigal Land, Suite 310, 46–56 Kippax Street, Surry Hills, NSW 2010, Australia
enquiries@currency.com.au
www.currency.com.au

in association with La Mama

Copyright: *Garage Girls* © Candace Miles, Madelaine Nunn and Anna Rodway, 2024.

COPYING FOR EDUCATIONAL PURPOSES

The Australian *Copyright Act 1968* [Act] allows a maximum of one chapter or 10% of this book, whichever is the greater, to be copied by any educational institution for its educational purposes provided that that educational institution [or the body that administers it] has given a remuneration notice to Copyright Agency [CA] under the Act.

For details of the CA licence for educational institutions contact CA, 12 / 66 Goulburn Street, Sydney, NSW, 2000; tel: within Australia 1800 066 844 toll free; outside Australia 61 2 9394 7600; fax: 61 2 9394 7601; email: memberservices@copyright.com.au

COPYING FOR OTHER PURPOSES

Except as permitted under the Act, for example a fair dealing for the purposes of study, research, criticism or review, no part of this book may be reproduced, stored in a retrieval system, or transmitted in any form or by any means without prior written permission. All enquiries should be made to the publisher at the address above.
Any performance or public reading of *Garage Girls* is forbidden unless a licence has been received from the author or the author's agent. The purchase of this book in no way gives the purchaser the right to perform the play in public, whether by means of a staged production or a reading. All applications for public performance should be addressed to the author c / —Currency Press

Typeset by Brighton Gray for Currency Press.
Cover image by Tony Rive.

Any queries relating to the reproduction of copyright material should be addressed to the publisher at the above address.

Currency Press acknowledges the Traditional Owners of the Country on which we live and work. We pay our respects to all Aboriginal and Torres Strait Islander Elders, past and present.

 A catalogue record for this book is available from the National Library of Australia

# Contents

GARAGE GIRLS 1

*Theatre Program at the end of the playtext*

*Garage Girls* was first produced by La Mama at La Mama Courthouse Theatre, on the traditional Land of the people of the Kulin Nation, Melbourne, on 24 April 2024 with the following cast and creatives:

| | |
|---|---|
| ALICE ANDERSON | Madelaine Nunn |
| MAGGIE / ELLEN MARY / ENSEMBLE | Carolyn Bock |
| RUTH / JT / ENSEMBLE | Helen Hopkins |
| FLEURY / FRANKIE / ENSEMBLE | Candace Miles |
| MARIE / JESSIE / ENSEMBLE | Anna Rodway |

Creators, Helen Hopkins, Carolyn Bock (The Shift Theatre), Candace Miles, Madelaine Nunn and Anna Rodway (Three Birds Theatre)
Direction and Production Dramaturgy, Janice Muller
Script Dramaturgy, Helen Hopkins and Carolyn Bock
Set and Costume Design, Sophie Woodward
Lighting Design, Gina Gascoigne
Sound Design, Rachel 'Stoz' Stone
Stage Management, Claire Shepherd
Set Construction, Jacob Battista

The creators acknowledge the inclusion of poems from *The Rubaiyat of Omar Khayyam* and Helen Truesdell.

# CHARACTERS

### Family
ALICE ANDERSON
JT
ELLEN MARY
FRANKIE
CLAIRE

### Garage Girls
RUTH
MAGGIE
MARIE
FLEURY

### Melbourne
JESSIE
REPORTER
RADIO VOICE
SUITOR
GARAGE MAN
BANK WOMAN
BANK MAN
MISS CATTACH
WORKER 1
WORKER 2
WORKER 3
WORKER 4
PASSERBY
MR TWOPENNY
MRS TWOPENNY
CUSTOMER 1
CUSTOMER 2
CUSTOMER 3
CUSTOMER 4

JOURNALIST 1
JOURNALIST 2
NEWS LADY
PARTY PERSON 1
PARTY PERSON 2
PARTY PERSON 3
PARTY PERSON 4
WOMAN 1
WOMAN 2
WOMAN 3
POLICEMAN
MECHANIC 1
MECHANIC 2

## Alice Springs
LOCAL 1
LOCAL 2
LOCAL 3
AMELIA EARHART
OODNADATTA MAN

## The Narrators
NARRATOR (1)
NARRATOR (2)
NARRATOR (3)
NARRATOR (4)

## NOTES ON TEXT

*Garage Girls* is a fictional re-imagining of the life of Alice Anderson. Inspiration for characters and story throughout this playscript has been sourced through archival research and the biography of Alice Anderson: *A Spanner in the Works* by Loretta Smith.

The story, all names, characters, and incidents portrayed in this production are a theatrical re-imagining of the life of Alice Anderson. Whilst real-life persons and names are used at times throughout the playscript, no accurate or definitive identification with actual persons (living or deceased), places, buildings, and products is intended or should be inferred.

The narration can be spoken or used as stage directions. This choice is at the discretion of the director.

A slash (/) indicates when the next actor should start speaking.

A dash (—) indicates an interruption or change in thought.

This play text went to press before the end of rehearsals and may differ from the play as performed.

## SCENE 1

NARRATOR (1): A starry night in Alice Springs.
NARRATOR (2): Light beams from the headlights of a motorcar.
NARRATOR (3): Desert sounds and the rumblings of distant thunder.
NARRATOR (4): This is Alice. Alice Anderson.

    ALICE *emerges.*

ALICE: It's an extraordinary pleasure, available to many ordinary people …
There's nothing else like it.
The click of the gear stick.
My hands on the wheel.
The roar beneath my bones.
The shudder.
The surge.
I'm off!
It's an atmosphere as exhilarating as wine, that makes me catch my breath, cheeks pink, as I speed in sheer joy at the goodness of life.
The wide-open road awaits.
The promise of a new day.

## SCENE 2

NARRATOR (3): It's 1920s Melbourne!
NARRATOR (4): The streets are alive with the sounds of trams,
NARRATOR (2): The clatter of the horse and carriage—
NARRATOR (3): And the roar of the motorcar!
NARRATOR (1): There's a spring in Alice's step, as she darts through the streets and arrives at a mechanic's garage …

    *A burly* MECHANIC *surveys* ALICE. *The remaining ensemble transforms into* GARAGE WORKERS.

GARAGE MAN: Name.
ALICE: Alecia Elizabeth Foley Anderson. Alice for short.
GARAGE MAN: Age.
ALICE: Twenty years and three-and-a-half months. Give or take a few days.

GARAGE MAN: And you want to work here?

ALICE: A dream.

GARAGE MAN: Well, the books need tidying and the boys love a cuppa in the morning—though you'd have to wear a frock, or a—

ALICE: I'm sorry to interrupt, but I'm actually here for the advertised position of mechanic.

GARAGE MAN: I beg your pardon?

ALICE: The advertised position of mechanic.

GARAGE MAN: I think there's been a misunderstanding.

ALICE: There's no misunderstanding. I have a rigorous and comprehensive working knowledge of the latest four-cylinder, including detailing and body repairs! I drove the Black Spur when I was eighteen, I am skilled with tools and I have the mind of an engineer. Or, so my father says!

GARAGE MAN: Listen, Miss Anderson—let me be frank—the mechanic's life is not for the likes of you.

ALICE: How so?

GARAGE MAN: There'd be too much swearing, for one.

*The* GARAGE WORKERS *guffaw.*

ALICE: Well, I wouldn't understand it.

GARAGE MAN: Little lady, I don't mean to be rude but …

ALICE: I can assure you, I am very serious!

GARAGE MAN: The answer's no.

ALICE: But—I've already been to all five garages in Hawthorn and they've all said no. Look, I'm ready to learn and, more importantly, ready to work.

GARAGE MAN: This ain't women's work.

## SCENE 3

NARRATOR (1): The English, Scottish and Australian Bank stands like an imposing fortress on the corner of Collins and Queen. A winding queue snakes its way along the polished marble floors.

NARRATOR (2): Finally, Alice is bumped to the front. She can barely see over the counter.

*The* BANK TELLERS *glare at* ALICE *inquisitively.*

ALICE: Excuse me. I'm here for a loan.

BANK MAN: WHO are you?
ALICE: I am an excellent candidate with a regular income. Or I will be. When you kindly award me a loan, that is.
BANK WOMAN: Name.
ALICE: Alecia Elizabeth Foley Anderson. Alice for short.
BANK MAN: Have you had a loan before?
ALICE: First time. First time for everything.
BANK WOMAN: Are you married, young—woman?
ALICE: No. Are you?
BANK MAN: I see. A rapier wit.
ALICE: Thank you.
BANK WOMAN: She's very small.
BANK MAN: Too small to handle a lump sum.
BANK WOMAN: Who is your guarantor?
ALICE: Guarantor?
BOTH BANK TELLERS: YES, a guarantor!
ALICE: I didn't realise I had to have a guarantor.
BANK WOMAN: [*laughing*] What? Didn't realise?
BANK MAN: Can you believe it?
BANK WOMAN: No husband—
BANK MAN: No income—
BOTH BANK TELLERS: No guarantor?!
ALICE: I was hoping to get this sorted by myself …
BANK WOMAN: Is there a Father Anderson?
BANK MAN: Brother Anderson?
ALICE: It's just me! But don't let that dissuade you! Picture this …

    ALICE *enters a moment of fantasy.*

Three storeys high—light streams through the skylight windows! Look down from above and what do you see? A row of newly washed cars, lined up for repair! A seven-seater Hupmobile sparkles in the sun! Ready for a tour on the wide-open road.

    A pristine workshop—so clean you could eat off the bench! An office to your left. A bookshelf to your right. Fresh flowers on the sill, just next to the lathe—a feminine touch!

    Young girls clamour to learn how to drive. Old girls clamour to learn how to drive. A line around the corner, just to see it for themselves!

> Announcing ... Miss Anderson's Motor Service—the first all-girl garage in the country!
>
> *The* BANK TELLERS *applaud.*

Now place it in the *Sun*!
BOTH TELLERS: Done!
ALICE: And the *Sands* and *McDougall's Directory*!
BOTH TELLERS: Done!
ALICE: Tell the neighbourhood! Miss Anderson's Motor Service is ready for—
BANK WOMAN: Earth to Alice!

> *The* BANK TELLERS *ring a bell, jerking* ALICE *back to reality.*

BANK MAN: Someone's fallen down the rabbit hole!
WOMAN: Send a telegram to Lewis Carroll—
BANK MAN: He wants his protagonist back!

> *The* BANK TELLERS *laugh in a hysterical yet orderly fashion.*

ALICE: So you'll grant me the loan, then?
BANK WOMAN: No husband.
BANK MAN: No loan.
BOTH: No garage.

## SCENE 4

*A memory.*

NARRATOR (2): The tinkling of bell birds and kookaburras herald in the Australian bush. Cicadas, the sounds of summer. We're in Narbethong, Alice's childhood home.
NARRATOR (3): The morning sun casts a bright glow across the plains of the Anderson property.

> JT *appears.*

NARRATOR (4): This is Joshua Thomas Anderson, JT for short—Alice's father.
JT: [*with an Irish lilt*] Happy eighteenth birthday, Alice!
ALICE: Not the Hups? Padded leather, wood-grain panelling ... Seven passengers—
JT: Thanks to that dickie seat!

ALICE: It's even got the family crest!
JT / ALICE: 'We Stoop Not'!
ALICE: She's big. Accelerator designed for a size-eleven foot … it'll be a stretch to reach.
JT: If anyone can do it, you can.
ALICE: And you'll teach me!
JT: You don't need teaching. It's in your blood.
ALICE: But how will I learn to drive?
JT: You've got the mind of an engineer, just like your father. I'll be busy darting about town for the next few months.
ALICE: But—?
JT: See those paddocks?

*He points to the horizon.*

Just practise out there—you'll be ready in no time.
ALICE: All right.

*She looks down at the car.*

ALICE: It's very generous of you, Da. Thank you.
JT: Gee, it's a beauty, isn't it? It's a great investment!
ALICE: Investment?
JT: You'll have to pay it off of course. Nothing comes for free, Alice. You know that. Those bookies down at Caulfield know that.
ALICE: [*tentatively*] How much?
JT: Only … four hundred and sixty pounds.
ALICE: Four hundred and sixty pounds?!
JT: I put down the deposit.
ALICE: How am I going to pay it off?
JT: You've got your whole life ahead of you, Alice. You'll think of something!

## SCENE 5

NARRATOR (3): On a brisk and biting Melbourne morning, Alice weaves her way by the convent, up over the river—
NARRATOR (1): —down Studley Park Road, past the boathouse—
NARRATOR (3): —through the Junction and finds herself in Cotham Road, Kew.

NARRATOR (4): She stands outside a shabby, wooden shed. A 'For Lease' sign hangs from the door. Alice is met by the landlady, Miss Cattach.

MISS CATTACH: [*with a thick, Scottish accent*] My brother would usually welcome new tenants but he's got the dreaded lurgy. Although he is very much better, complaining only of a husky throat! Well, this is it.

ALICE: Oh, it's … smaller than the newspaper described it to be …

MISS CATTACH: You won't find a roomier place in the whole of Kew.

ALICE: The window pane is broken …

MISS CATTACH: A hairline crack. As thin as my finger!

ALICE: How draughty does it get in winter?

MISS CATTACH: Winter? Practically summer compared to the Scottish Highlands!

ALICE: I'll need to have the floors asphalted and the doors put on hinges.

MISS CATTACH: Any kind of luxury upgrade must be paid for by the tenant.

ALICE: It's not perfect but it does have potential.

MISS CATTACH: My thoughts exactly.

ALICE: It won't fit six motorcars, but I'm sure I could start with two.

MISS CATTACH: Motorcars? What on earth are you going to do with motorcars?

ALICE: Fix them! Drive them. Tour them.

MISS CATTACH: All that in my shack?

ALICE: Don't you mean your 'garden-view investment opportunity'?

MISS CATTACH: Yes! I mean to say, my garden-view investment opportunity! I thought you were opening a millinery?

ALICE: A millinery? In these pants, Miss Cattach? I don't think so.

MISS CATTACH: Well, I might have to reconsider this proposal.

ALICE: Reconsider?

MISS CATTACH: What would the neighbours think?

ALICE: Hats are for heads. Motorcars are for the future!

MISS CATTACH: There's nothing a motorcar can do that a penny farthing can't.

ALICE: That's where you're wrong, Miss Cattach. Believe me, I will be an exemplary tenant!

MISS CATTACH: You do know, it's got a hole in the roof.

ALICE: I'll have it fixed in a jiff!

MISS CATTACH: And there is a nasty draught in winter!

ALICE: Nothing compared to the Scottish Highlands! From one business owner to the next, Miss Cattach. I could be a long-lasting tenant.

    MISS CATTACH *hesitates.*

MISS CATTACH: I don't know …
ALICE: And I have the money upfront!
MISS CATTACH: Upfront! Well, I never. The bank gave you a loan, then?

    *Small pause.*

ALICE: Something of the sort.
MISS CATTACH: So long as there's no funny business. I lead a simple life, you know.
ALICE: You won't regret it!
MISS CATTACH: The rent is due the first Thursday of the month and I don't grant favours.
ALICE: And I don't accept them.
MISS CATTACH: It's agreed. If you see my brother—don't tell him I'm off to the races. Toodaloo!

    MISS CATTACH *exits.*

ALICE: [*to herself*] Nothing ventured, nothing gained.

## SCENE 6

*Sunshine streams through the hole in the roof. There is a hubbub of movement as the garage is built, brick by brick.* ALICE *bosses* WORKERS *around the space.*

WORKER 1: Bricks for Miss Anderson?
ALICE: Stack at the rear!
WORKER 2: An order of timber?
ALICE: Next to the lathe.
WORKER 3: Glass for the windows?
ALICE: Second on the left.
    No grease inside! Watch the machinery!
WORKER 4: Tin for the roof?
ALICE: Finally!
WORKER 2: A box of locks, Miss Anderson?
ALICE: Out with the old and in with the new!

*SCENE 7*

NARRATOR (3): After three months of toil—night and day, no sleep, no rest—

NARRATOR (2): There are tools on the bench, her name on the door … finally Miss Anderson's Motor Service is open for business.

NARRATOR (1): Alice waits alone inside the garage. No customers.

NARRATOR (3): No-one arrives. Not the next week. Or the week after that.

NARRATOR (2): Or, the week after that …

NARRATOR (4): … if a tumbleweed could roll by, it would.

NARRATOR (1): But wait! The sound of footsteps!

*A* PASSERBY *approaches.* ALICE *accosts him.*

ALICE: [*eagerly*] Welcome, sir! Is that your Cleveland parked over there?

PASSERBY: What is it to you?

ALICE: I can have that cracked headlight fixed!

PASSERBY: What?

ALICE: Or the body polished?

PASSERBY: I think not!

ALICE: A tour then! Through the rolling hills of Daylesford? Complimentary scones and cream?

PASSERBY: I'll take the scones but hang the tour.

ALICE: Well, you only get the scones if you go on the tour.

PASSERBY: [*scoffing*] With who? With you?

ALICE: Why, yes—with me!

PASSERBY: I don't know what you're talking about, young man. I've got an appointment at the courthouse and thanks to you, I'm lost!

ALICE: My apologies, sir. Continue down this road and take a right at High.

PASSERBY *tries to disentangle himself and begins to walk away.*

But if you have a motorcar that needs fixing, you know where to come!

PASSERBY *exits.*

ALICE *is left alone again.*

## SCENE 8

*A memory. Narbethong.* ALICE *is in bed with her sisters,* CLAIRE *and* FRANKIE. *In the darkness, they sing to bring comfort to one another.*

ALL: [*singing*]
>The lambs in the green hills they sport as they play,
>And lots of strawberries grow round the salt sea,
>And lots of strawberries grow round the salt sea,
>And many's the ship sails the ocean.

CLAIRE: When will Mother and Father be back?
ALICE: In the morning.
CLAIRE: It's scary out here.
ALICE: Fear is useful! You just need to know where to put it.
CLAIRE: But I know that you will be gone soon, back to the city—
ALICE: Quiet now.
CLAIRE: And you'll never come home—
ALICE: Close your eyes, Claire.
FRANKIE: We know you, Alice. We know you don't let go of your dreams.
ALICE: What about your dreams, Frankie? I've seen you frolicking amongst the lavender bushes with a paintbrush in your hand.
FRANKIE: That's not the same.
ALICE: How's it different?
FRANKIE: Isn't it enough that I paint for myself?
ALICE: It wouldn't be fair—God has given you this gift—you must share it.
FRANKIE: Well … if I might dare to imagine … I would love a studio of my own some day—making artworks for Mother, to hang all over the house.
ALICE: Don't stop at Mother. Your work could hang in the finest galleries all over the country.
FRANKIE: Do you think so?
ALICE: I know so. But the first step to a dream is sleep.

SCENE 9

NARRATOR (3): Alice steps into the hall of the *Argus Daily Newspaper*, at the Paris end of Collins Street.

JOURNALIST 1: Would you believe it! PM Billy Hughes was spotted on the corner of Bourke and Elizabeth devouring an éclair!

JOURNALIST 2: I need that story by noon! And not a second later or I'll have your head.

NEWS LADY: [*to* ALICE] Do you need something?

ALICE: I'd like to place an ad. For Miss Anderson's Motor Service.

NEWS LADY: When you're ready.

    ALICE *clears her throat. Heads snap towards her.*

ALICE: Miss Anderson's Motor Service
COMMA,
Cotham Road Kew
COMMA,
is proud to offer her touring cars for hire
STOP.
No place too far
STOP.
NEW LINE:
Petrol
COMMA,
tyres
COMMA,
and all motor accessories
STOP.
Repairs to all classes of cars
STOP.
Signing off Alice F. Anderson
STOP.
Three pounds seventy. I want the ad running for a month!

## SCENE 10

*The garage. Two weeks later.* ALICE *is startled by the arrival of an older, 'well-to-do' couple.*

MR TWOPENNY *is a proud and inquisitive gentleman. His wife,* MRS TWOPENNY, *is a sweet and girlish woman, with her mouth in a permanently open state.*

*Arm-in-arm,* MR TWOPENNY *steers himself and* MRS TWOPENNY *into the garage.*

MR TWOPENNY: Here we are, darling.
MRS TWOPENNY: Are you sure this is the right address?

    ALICE *emerges.*

ALICE: Welcome to Cotham Road Kew.
MR TWOPENNY: Richard Twopenny.
ALICE: Alice Anderson.

    *She gestures to* MRS TWOPENNY.

And—Mrs Twopenny?
MRS TWOPENNY: My friends call me Betsy.
ALICE: My friends call me Alice.
MR TWOPENNY: So it's true! We saw your ad in the paper.
MRS TWOPENNY: We thought it was a misprint.
MR TWOPENNY: Wanted to see it for ourselves.
ALICE: So that's your Dodge Sedan parked out the front.
MR TWOPENNY: You know it then?
ALICE: Yes sir, stylish and solid air pressure. Very reliable.
MR TWOPENNY: I think so, too.
ALICE: I've always said one's character is reflected in their choice of motor vehicle.
MR TWOPENNY: Yes, quite right.
ALICE: Now, what seems to be the problem, sir?
MR TWOPENNY: I would usually visit Brothers and Toms but I was unable to make a reservation. There's an absolutely alarming rattle. I wouldn't trust it to get us to Prahran in one piece.
MRS TWOPENNY: It's a short route to a migraine.

ALICE: I know how dreadful they can be. My mother is prone to such ailments. Miss Cattach—

    MISS CATTACH *bustles forward.*

One cup of tea and some smelling salts for Mrs Betsy Twopenny.

MISS CATTACH: Yes, Miss Alice, on the double!

ALICE: I can have your Dodge ready for you by four o'clock this afternoon.

MR TWOPENNY: So soon? What a speedy turnaround.

ALICE: Better yet—I'll have it done by four and I'll give you the 'Once-Over' with no extra cost.

MRS TWOPENNY: What on earth is a 'Once-Over'?

ALICE: I'm glad you asked, Betsy. [*To audience*] It is my own initiative. I'll have the gearbox and battery inspected, radiator drained, flushed and refilled, tyres checked and those loose nuts tightened.

MRS TWOPENNY: Do you operate here alone, Miss Anderson?

ALICE: Yes, I'm proud to say I'm the sole mechanic on the premises.

MRS TWOPENNY: How unusual.

ALICE: Perhaps you'll even get behind the wheel, Betsy.

    MRS TWOPENNY *laughs, shrilly.*

MRS TWOPENNY: I couldn't possibly! I can't drive!

ALICE: I could teach you!

MR TWOPENNY: What a novel idea!

## SCENE 11

NARRATOR (2): Word hits the Melbourne streets, thanks to the Twopennys. A flurry of customers descend upon the garage.

ALICE: Caster is good. Camber is good. Kingpin inclination and toe-in on specification. No marks on the axle. No impact on the spring pads.

CUSTOMER 1: Thank you, Miss Anderson!

CUSTOMER 2: What seems to be the problem?

ALICE: The problem stems from a bent chassis and a crooked rear axle. No wonder you're crab-walking down the road.

CUSTOMER 3: The engine isn't sparking—

ALICE: I'll have it ready by Tuesday.

CUSTOMER 4: My Packard is smoking—
ALICE: Ready by Wednesday—
CUSTOMER 2: There's a putrid smell from my Hudson—
CUSTOMER 1: The Mercer's wheels are wobbling—
CUSTOMER 3: My beautiful blue Summit!
ALICE: I'll work through the weekend!

SCENE 12

*Back at the newspaper office ...*

JOURNALIST 1: Would you believe it! Dame Nellie Melba caught in frisson with famous flautist!
JOURNALIST 2: I need that story by noon and not a second later or I'll have your head.
NEWS LADY: Back again!

    ALICE *clears her throat. Heads snap towards her.*

ALICE: Miss Anderson's Motor Service is now seeking staff
STOP.
Looking for girls with eight years of education
COMMA,
She must be in a position to undertake any repairs
COMMA,
With a working knowledge of trig
STOP.
My ambition is to turn a trade into a profession for women
STOP
Signing off, Alice F. Anderson
STOP.

SCENE 13

*The garage. Night.* ALICE *is seated, her head is bowed.*

NARRATOR (1): Alice is finally alone, at the end of a long day.
NARRATOR (3): She locks the doors and extinguishes the lamps—
NARRATOR (4): Before retreating to her cupboard at the back of the workshop.

NARRATOR (2): Small for some people, but a perfect sleeping nook for Alice.

ALICE: [*whispering, to herself*] I thank you this day,
For your grace, your provision,
Help me hold firm in my faith—

*ALICE hears an engine rumble. She looks up for a moment, then returns to prayer.*

Bless Ma, bless Da, bless Frankie and Claire.
Bless—

*ALICE hears footsteps. She stands. A beam of light slowly scans through the garage window.*

Is anyone there?

*The moment hangs.*

## SCENE 14

*Morning, the next day.* RUTH SNELL *enters the garage, dressed smartly for an interview. She looks a touch uncomfortable in her attire. She carries herself with confidence, despite her innate awkwardness.*

RUTH: Ruth Snell. I read about you in the *Argus*. I was too nervous to apply sooner.

*She looks around the space.*

Goodness, it's much bigger in here than I expected.

ALICE: There's been overwhelming interest in the position. Why, just today, seven girls have come past to enquire—

MISS CATTACH *pokes head in.*

MISS CATTACH: Miss Alice, no-one's come past but the milkman—

ALICE: Could you please fetch us some tea, Miss Cattach?

MISS CATTACH *scurries away.*

Well, Snell. Why are you interested in this line of work?

RUTH: A few reasons—I've allergies to the department-store perfumes.

ALICE: Go on.

RUTH: I'm not a strong speller.

ALICE: I see. Education is essential. I'd prefer eight years.

RUTH: Eight years?
ALICE: But for the right person, I'm willing to make an exception. You must be in a position to undertake / any repairs.
RUTH: Any repairs COMMA, with a working knowledge of trig STOP. Your ambition is to turn a trade into a profession for women STOP.

> *Beat.* ALICE *is impressed.*

ALICE: You do know it's dirty work: washing and greasing.
RUTH: I'm no stranger to dirty work.
ALICE: It'll be early mornings and late nights.
RUTH: I'm a night owl and a morning lark.
ALICE: It'll be long hours and no overtime.
RUTH: I expect nothing less. It's better than selling coat hangers and watch straps.
ALICE: [*to audience*] I can't argue with that.
RUTH: Please, Miss Anderson. You won't regret it.
ALICE: Well if you're up for it: the lavatory will always be clean, the coffee will always be hot and if you're doing what you love, you'll never work a day in your life. We'll make the work count!
RUTH: Too right!
ALICE: Come back tomorrow at half-six. Wear trousers and a crisp white shirt.

## SCENE 15

MAGGIE DODD *enters, with a laugh in her voice and a spring in her step.*

MAGGIE: [*with enthusiasm*] Maggie Dodd.
ALICE: What inspired you to apply for the position, Dodd?
MAGGIE: The thought of sitting on a sofa all day waiting for a proposal from a suitor?

> MAGGIE *laughs.*

I'd rather the leather upholstery ... and my foot on the clutch.
ALICE: So you're not planning on getting married.
MAGGIE: No. Vowed I never would.
ALICE: And do you drive?
MAGGIE: Yes. Both a buggy and a motorcar. I'm also an accomplished horsewoman.

ALICE: Ah! I'm a horsewoman myself. Winnie was my first love.
MAGGIE: What breed?
ALICE: A thoroughbred. Yours?
MAGGIE: Same. Retired racehorse. Ned Kelly.
ALICE: Ned Kelly! Was he just as troublesome?
MAGGIE: Like you wouldn't believe!
ALICE: Then you're no stranger to discipline and hard work.
MAGGIE: Up before dawn and last at the dinner table.
ALICE: You're a bit of a cracker, Dodd. I think we're going to get on. [*Calling* RUTH *over*] Snell! [*Gesturing*] Snell—Dodd.
MAGGIE: Dodd.
RUTH: Snell.
ALICE: Alice.
RUTH: Dodd.
MAGGIE: Snell.
ALICE: Alice.
MAGGIE: Dodd.
ALICE: We run a tight ship here, Dodd.
RUTH: Watertight!
MAGGIE: Well, giddy-up!

*SCENE 16*

*Enter* MARIE EDIE. *A young, wide-eyed ingénue, clasping her hat nervously in her hand.*

MARIE: Marie Edie.
ALICE: Anything else I ought to be aware of, Marie?
MARIE: [*blurts*] I'm a vegetarian.
ALICE: How avant-garde.
MARIE: I apologise. That's not relevant.
ALICE: I must admit I'm partial to a Sunday roast. But I respect your resolve.
MARIE: [*confused*] My resolve?
ALICE: … To be vegetarian.
MARIE: Oh, yes!
ALICE: So the working day begins at six and ends at six.
MARIE: Six.

ALICE: Is this going to be a problem?
MARIE: It's just ... The Palais starts jazz at six.
ALICE: They do say it's fashionable to be late—
MARIE: True!
ALICE: *Except* when working here.
MARIE: Understood.
ALICE: Now, you have no experience—no time behind the wheel—and no formal qualifications.
MARIE: Yes! But I'll do anything you ask.
ALICE: I will take you on as an apprentice. Your first job—polishing.
MARIE: Motorcars?
ALICE: Spoons.

SCENE 17

*Enter* FLEURY. *Curt, sophisticated and 'very French'.*

FLEURY: Gabrielle de Fleurelle.
ALICE: Right, Fleury it is.
FLEURY: I have three years of driving from my time in the war.
ALICE: Impressive. Which unit were you under?
FLEURY: The British Women's Land Army. I drove tractors and trucks through country roads. I can fix anything with wheels!
ALICE: What brought you to Melbourne?
FLEURY: I needed a change.
ALICE: Fair enough. You'll make an excellent chauffeuse.
FLEURY: Give me a map and I'll go where you need, Miss Anderson!
ALICE: That's the spirit! And call me Alice.

SCENE 18

ALICE *takes the* GARAGE GIRLS *through their training.*

ALICE: In the Buick carburetor, the float chamber surrounds the asperator, which is in the form of ...
RUTH: [*with nervousness*] A hollow tube.
ALICE: Correct. It has very small ... ?
MARIE: [*with delight*] Holes!
ALICE: And where are they?

MARIE: In the side … toward the intake pipe of the engine.
ALICE: Correct! So the air coming into the carburetor strikes …
RUTH: A hinged plane!
ALICE: Which is raised or lowered as …
MAGGIE: [*with excitement*] The amount of air is increased or decreased.
ALICE: Correct! This hinged plane is connected with—
FLEURY: [*with 'French' confidence*] The hollow aspirator tube, which rises and falls with it as the quantity of air changes. So, more of the holes are uncovered and more petroleum is drawn into the intake pipe.
ALICE: Touché! If you can see it, you can fix it. Dodd, turn to page fifty-eight of Dykes.
MAGGIE: Righto!
ALICE: Snell, dig out the biscuits.

## SCENE 19

*The streets of Kew. A driving lesson.* MARIE *is in the driver's seat,* ALICE *in the passenger side.* ALICE *coaches her along.* FLEURY, MAGGIE *and* RUTH *are in the backseat.*

MARIE *screams.*

ALICE: Eyes open, Marie! Left.
MARIE: But I'm afraid!
FLEURY: You're afraid of your left shoe!
ALICE: Left!

> *They jerk left.*

Focus! Ten to two—

> *They jerk forwards, then backwards.*

MAGGIE: Marie, I'm going to lose my lunch!
ALICE: Foot on the clutch! Pedal to the metal!

> *They lurch backwards, then forwards.*

RUTH: What if we get lost?
ALICE: Never admit to your passengers that you don't know where you are.
FLEURY: What do we say, then?

ALICE: You're taking the scenic route!
RUTH: A short cut!
MAGGIE: A trip down Memory Lane?
ALICE: And always bring home the bacon, Marie.
MARIE: But I'm a vegetarian!
ALICE: Book them in for their next drive before this one's finished! Tight, tight, tight—
RUTH: Watch the junction!
MARIE: Which way?
MAGGIE: Princess!     RUTH: High!     FLEURY: Denmark!
ALICE: Watch the tram!

*The furious 'dinging' of a tram.*

## SCENE 20

*A bustling day at the garage. The telephone rings.*

NARRATOR (2): Six months later. Miss Anderson's Motor Service is a well-oiled machine, with business snapping at its heels.

*MARIE emerges.*

MARIE: Alice, it's the Dovers family. They need their Summit by two o'clock instead of three! They're heading off to Queenscliff!
ALICE: We'll have it done by two!

*MARIE disappears. The telephone rings again.*

RUTH: Alice, it's stuck—it's stuck!
FLEURY: Put your back into it, Snell!
MARIE: Alice, it's Mrs Redwing. She needs her daughter picked up from Miss M. Lindsay Ladies' Hairdressing and Toilet Parlour!
ALICE: Right you are—Fleury, take the Elgin!
FLEURY: Allons-y!
MAGGIE: Alice! Mr Bradshaw's Daimler has arrived. Hit right up the rear by a tram on Commercial.
ALICE: Start with a drop test. Then do a wheelbase check.
MAGGIE: Right-o!

*The telephone rings once more.*

RUTH: Alice, it's still stuck!

ALICE: Twist it twice to the left and yank it with a crowbar if you have to!

MARIE: Alice!

ALICE: Yes?

MARIE: It's your mother!

ALICE: Take a message, Marie—I can hardly understand why she thinks I have the time to talk!

## SCENE 21

NARRATOR (1): Not everyone is impressed with Miss Anderson's Motor Service.

NARRATOR (2): Times are changing too fast for some people ...

*A* POLICEMAN *enters.*

POLICEMAN: Noise pollution, oil dumping—

ALICE: Well, officer, this is a working garage—

POLICEMAN: —Odious petrol scent, grease marks through the local streets—there've been complaints!

ALICE: Officer, are you inspecting all the garages in the precinct?

POLICEMAN: This girl [*gestures to* FLEURY] running amuck, speeding all over town—

FLEURY: I was not!

POLICEMAN: Scaring the horses!

ALICE: Horses are notoriously spooked, which is why the motorcar—

POLICEMAN: Since the likes of you have come along, all we get called out to are accidents.

ALICE: We're not the only ones on the road!

POLICEMAN: It's a dangerous game you're playing—dressed the way you dress, doing what you do. Just today I was on the Esplanade, there was a mighty collision!

ALICE: And I am just as horrified as the next person, officer! But we can't deny automobiles are here to stay, and my garage is not the cause.

POLICEMAN: Listen, Miss Anderson. If I get called out here one more time you'll be facing a hefty fine. Do not doubt, it would give me great pleasure to shut this freak show down.

ALICE: I'd like to see you try!

## SCENE 22

NARRATOR (1): A few weeks later. Alice is on the 'get-out-and-get-under'.

NARRATOR (3): An invention of her own, we might add.

NARRATOR (1): A nervous, but unknowingly charming young man hovers next to her.

    *The* GARAGE GIRLS *watch the unfolding interaction with glee.*

ALICE: You see, the bearing was off-kilter because of the darn pothole on Burke Road.

SUITOR: I'm still marvelling at the polish. Thank you, Miss Anderson.

ALICE: Oh, that was Marie's doing.

    MARIE *waves flirtatiously.*

It's a beauty, this model. When did it come into your possession?

SUITOR: It was a gift from my father.

ALICE: And did you have to pay it off too?

SUITOR: [*confused*] Pardon?

ALICE: Never mind. What a generous gift.

SUITOR: You know, I didn't realise it'd be true.

ALICE: About what?

SUITOR: About you, Miss Alice—your enthusiasm and pluck and unwavering knowledge of the automobile. You're precariously clever!

ALICE: Well, I always like to be one step ahead.

MAGGIE: [*calling*] You can say that again!

SUITOR: If it's not presumptuous of me—would Saturday next suit?

ALICE: Saturday next? You're interested in our new 'Ballarat Backstreets Tour'?

SUITOR: [*confused—again*] I beg your pardon?

ALICE: Twenty pounds for the weekend. Picnic lunch. Champagne! An informative outing through the blue gums and valley roads. [*To audience*] We're the only ones offering it.

SUITOR: Oh! Ah, no—although that does sound grand—it's just—there's a matinee of *Pirates of Penzance* at the Princess Theatre. On Saturday.

ALICE: On Saturday … I'm sure one of the girls would be happy to be your chauffeuse!

    ALICE *gestures towards* MARIE. MARIE*'s eyes widen.*

SUITOR: Ah—no. Sorry, Miss Anderson—I'll be frank.

ALICE: Frank?

SUITOR: Ah. No—[*points to self*] George.

ALICE: George … ?

SUITOR: But my brother's name is Frank … In any case, I'd be exceedingly obliged if you would join me at the theatre. As my guest.

    *Small pause.*

ALICE: I am fond of Gilbert and Sullivan—although I must apologise—my schedule is confirmed and I couldn't possibly leave the garage at such short notice.

SUITOR: Not a worry. How's the week after next?

ALICE: I really couldn't say.

SUITOR: Well, no harm. I eagerly await my next 'Once-Over'. Thank you, again.

ALICE: [*embarrassed*] Any time!

    *The* SUITOR *exits. The* GARAGE GIRLS *hoot with laughter.*

[*Feigning naivety*] What?

RUTH: Alice, did you see that gold watch on his wrist?

MARIE: I'd die if a man of that stature looked at me the way he just looked at you.

MAGGIE: That's the third proposal—what was wrong with that one?

ALICE: Nothing. He was perfectly charming.

MARIE: He even smelt nice.

MAGGIE: Not like my sweaty shirt!

MARIE: Perhaps you'll get married some day! If only for a rest.

ALICE: A rest, is that what you call it? I think it is only a change of work. What's next? He smuggles me from the theatre to his house and then I'm trapped there forever, darning socks and baking bread!

MAGGIE: Alice is right—my married friends have never stopped crying.

ALICE: Not to mention the debt!

RUTH: Debt? What do you mean, Alice?

ALICE: [*ignoring* RUTH] I've got too many things to do before I get married!
FLEURY: You don't have to marry or have children, but don't you long for someone of your own?
ALICE: I've got all of you. I've got this. And we are doing something here. I wouldn't give that up for a gold watch. Nor a hairy back.

*SCENE 23*

*Night.* ALICE *is alone in the garage. The telephone rings.*

ALICE: Alice Anderson's Motor Service?

> *Silence.*

Alice Anderson's Motor Service?

> ALICE *hears breathing through the receiver.*

Hello?
> Is anyone there?

> *She waits.*

Stop ringing me!

> ALICE *thrusts the receiver back in its place.*

*SCENE 24*

*Christmas time. A* REPORTER *makes notes outside 88 Cotham Rd: the grand opening of the new and expanded premises for Miss Anderson's Motor Service. An enthusiastic crowd of locals hailing from Kew, Malvern, Toorak and the like, gather around.*

REPORTER: [*to crowd*] Success comes to some women early in life. Take, for instance, little Alice Anderson, of Melbourne, who is still on the very sunny side of thirty, and who, through her own enterprise, persistence, and hard work, has become the first woman garage proprietor in Australasia. From humble beginnings in a backyard shed, Miss Anderson is now proud to open her new bespoke and pristine premises. And the fact that Alice employs only girl chauffeurs makes her business possibly unique in the world!
ALICE: Welcome to eighty-eight Cotham Road, Kew!

REPORTER: What inspired you to set up such an establishment?

ALICE: My ambition is to turn a trade into a profession for women and it is well within the grasp of those with initiative and grit.

REPORTER: What's a typical day in the garage?

ALICE: Girls—

MAGGIE: We start every morning with a cup of English breakfast tea—God save the King!

FLEURY: We mend punctures, do mechanical repairs—

MARIE: —attend to telephone calls—

ALICE: —not to mention our especially tailored driving lessons for women!

REPORTER: What does the future look like?

ALICE: It's bright. We're expanding—

MARIE: We are?

ALICE: We've had over fifty mothers trying to place their daughters in apprenticeships since Christmas.

MAGGIE: An inspiration!

ALICE: Our main client is the young girl. Mothers want to be secure in the knowledge that their daughter is in the care of a responsible woman. We are both chauffeuse and chaperone.

REPORTER: The other garages in the neighbourhood can't be happy?

ALICE: Nothing ventured, nothing gained. You can write that down.

FLEURY: We manage the entire business ourselves, under Alice.

REPORTER: This is remarkable! As the automobile takes off in Melbourne, proprietors such as Miss Anderson will surely be needed, as we step into a future where women really aren't purely ornamental!

*REPORTER gestures to the* GARAGE GIRLS.

May we take a photograph of you, Miss Alice? Out the front, if you please?

ALICE: Let's have one of the whole group.

*The* GARAGE GIRLS *pose once—twice, then—*

Flash them a smile, girls!

*The* GARAGE GIRLS *pose for the image.*

## SCENE 25

NARRATOR (4): The Lyceum Club: an exclusive Melbourne society for groundbreaking women.

NARRATOR (2): To the right, a discussion on medicine and Monet. To the left, Alice and her mother, Ellen Mary, sip tea.

ELLEN MARY: What will the ladies think?

ALICE: I'm sure they'd be impressed by my entrepreneurial spirit.

ELLEN MARY: How are you going to attract a suitor dressed like an undertaker's assistant?

ALICE: Oh, Mother.

ELLEN MARY: Do you have any understanding with any young man?

ALICE: The answer to your question need not worry you—or anyone else for that matter.

ELLEN MARY: What happens if you break your back under the bonnet of one of those things, what happens then?

ALICE: Are you questioning my skills, Mother?

ELLEN MARY: No, Alice, but you can't deny this unconventional work set-up is … off-putting.

ALICE: I know what I'm doing.

ELLEN MARY: You haven't looked this sickly since the boat back from Dunedin.

ALICE: I've never slept well, you know that.

ELLEN MARY: You can't deceive me, Alice. You have the same face as your father when plagued with money troubles.

ALICE: Who says there are money troubles? You say there are money troubles. I tire of talking at length about money troubles. I would appreciate a more supportive conversation.

*A very long pause.*

ELLEN MARY: Alice, I can sense you're upset. We will pause this discourse for another time. But my parting, sage advice is: keep your finances in order … and consider Mary Brandon's eldest son. I hear he is quite the catch.

*They wave in synchronisation at a woman across the room,* ALICE *through gritted teeth.*

ALICE: And is he threatened by a girl with gumption?
ELLEN MARY: Oh Alice. They all are.

## SCENE 26

NARRATOR (2): In a sunlit street by the Melbourne Public Library, Alice's path unexpectedly crosses with another's …

> ALICE *is peering at the building numbers when she bumps into an elegant woman, clutching a stack of books.*

ALICE: Oh, I am / sorry—
JESSIE: I didn't see / you—
ALICE: Let me help you with / that—
JESSIE: Thank you.
ALICE: [*noticing the book*] You have *The Collected Works of Keats.*
JESSIE: Yes—my copy is quite dog-eared, don't look too closely!
ALICE: I'd be concerned if it wasn't!

> *They laugh.*

JESSIE: Are you going somewhere?
ALICE: I'm meeting a … friend at the Windsor Hotel.
JESSIE: How lovely—The Duchess of Spring Street! Although I'm not sure they'll let you in dressed like a garage hand.
ALICE: I am a garage hand.
JESSIE: Oh. So you know Miss Anderson then?
ALICE: Know her? I … Of course I know her.
JESSIE: What's she like? I've been hoping to bump into her at the Lyceum Club, but as luck would have it, we keep missing each other.
ALICE: Well … she's excellent company. The life of the party. Not to mention an avid reader. Actually, I believe Keats is one of her favourites.
JESSIE: She sounds marvellous.
ALICE: She is.
JESSIE: Do you think I could trouble you to arrange an introduction?
ALICE: I don't know, she is in high demand, she doesn't usually take calls from—

> MR TWOPENNY *and* MRS TWOPENNY *float past.*

MR TWOPENNY: My sincerest gratitude for the work you did on my Dodge, Miss Anderson! The engine's purring like a pussycat!

ALICE: Any time, Mr Twopenny. [*Calling after them*] Betsy, don't forget your driving lessons!

    MRS TWOPENNY *laughs, giddily.*

    ALICE *turns back sheepishly to* JESSIE.

Alice Anderson.

    ALICE *extends her hand.* JESSIE *takes it.*

JESSIE: Jessie Webb. So how about that introduction, Miss Anderson?

## SCENE 27

NARRATOR (1): Early morning. Two rival mechanics lurk inside Alice's garage.

    ALICE *stops in her tracks.*

ALICE: What are you doing in here?
MECHANIC 1: Heard so much about this place.
MECHANIC 2: Bigger than I thought, Don.
ALICE: How'd you get in?
MECHANIC 1: She's even got Joe McBriety's Studebaker in here, Bill.
ALICE: How did you get in?
MECHANIC 1: We heard you were housing Sammy's Bentley, too.

    MECHANIC 2 *whistles.*

MECHANIC 2: That's some car.
MECHANIC 1: Worth a pretty penny.
MECHANIC 2: More than a thousand pounds isn't it, Don?
MECHANIC 1: Leaving it in the hands of girls—that's awfully trusting of him …
MECHANIC 2: I know, I wouldn't be so foolish.
ALICE: I've had no complaints.
MECHANIC 1: [*with innuendo*] Exactly what kind of services do you provide?
ALICE: A service you can't provide, clearly.
MECHANIC 2: We loved reading about you in the paper—
MECHANIC 1: Miss Anderson, you seem to know people in such high places—
MECHANIC 2: And low places.

ALICE: I don't know what you're talking about.
MECHANIC 1: I think you do.
ALICE: It's time for you to leave or I'll—
MECHANIC 2: Or you'll what?

> *A tense moment.*
>
> RUTH *and* MARIE *fall through the door.*

MARIE: Sorry we're late, Alice.
ALICE: Don't mind these gents, they were just leaving.
MECHANIC 1: Just a friendly hello from the boys at Dennys.
MECHANIC 2: I'm sure this won't be our last visit. Ladies …

> *The* MECHANICS *slowly exit. The* GARAGE GIRLS *share a look.*

## SCENE 28

RADIO VOICE: 'Who'd have thought we'd find ourselves in the grips of another wave of the Spanish Flu. Interstate trade and travel are nearly brought to a standstill again by the Commonwealth. Avoid crowds, observe personal cleanliness, keep in the sunshine, and prevent spitting and dirty habits. Most doctors say overindulging in alcohol is a danger.'
FLEURY: Are you sure I'm infected?
ALICE: You're burning up, Fleury!
FLEURY: I've barely got a cough. An ordinary cold.
MAGGIE: Don't come near me.
RUTH: Another cancellation, Alice.
ALICE: Have those parts from Newcastle arrived yet?
MARIE: Everything is at a standstill.
FLEURY: [*dramatically*] What's going to happen to me?
MARIE: They might send you back to France.
ALICE: You need to rest and keep up your fluids. Go home, Fleury.
FLEURY: I'm fine. I'm not missing the tour out to Warburton today.
ALICE: I'll do it.
RUTH: But you're fixing the sedan.
ALICE: I'll work through the night.
MAGGIE: Oh Alice, not again.
MARIE: Surely, we can just delay its return?

ALICE: Absolutely not. We can't afford to lose any more customers. Go home, Fleury. Snell—did they say how long?
RUTH: No, Alice. The ports are closed. Nothing's coming in and nothing's going out.
MAGGIE: How are we going to work?
ALICE: We'll make the tools if we have to. We've come through this once, we'll come through it again.

*SCENE 29*

*A memory.*

NARRATOR (2): We're back in Narbethong, in the depths of winter.
NARRATOR (4): Alice, still a child, is hiding, listening.
ELLEN MARY: What kind of business, JT?
JT: The bridge build is already underway. I'll be gone for a little while.
ELLEN MARY: You've only just arrived back home!
JT: Monash and I have secured contracts in Melbourne, Geelong and Bendigo.
ELLEN MARY: So you'll be everywhere but here.
JT: This one's going to work out, El.
ELLEN MARY: That's what you said about the last idea.
JT: That only didn't work out because they wouldn't take a chance. They were too small-minded.

*He grins to* ALICE.

Never be a small-minded person, Alice.
ALICE: [*from her hiding place*] I won't!
ELLEN MARY: Alice, go to bed. At least assure me this work will be paid in advance.
JT: We're still smoothing out the details.
ELLEN MARY: [*furtively*] There's only so much money I can squirrel away for myself and the girls. We're living off crumbs! When you brought us out here, to the middle of nowhere, you promised us a better life.
JT: And it will be a better life. This project is full of grand ideas. Alice, you'd love it!

ALICE *leaps out from her hiding place.*

ALICE: Then take me with you, Da!
JT: That's not half a bad idea.
ALICE: I could be your apprentice!
ELLEN MARY: I said—go to bed! [*To* JT] Who's going to make sure the house is kept warm this winter? The property's in complete disrepair!
JT: Alice can manage it.
ELLEN MARY: She has school.
JT: She can do both!
ALICE: I can do both!
ELLEN MARY: She's just a girl.
JT: She's nearly fully grown.
ELLEN MARY: She needs to focus on her education!
ALICE: I already know everything they're teaching me, Ma!
JT: The brightest spark in her class! She'll be fine.
ELLEN MARY: Fourteen crates of books crossed the seas with me so that she could read them all. We agreed the girls would have an education more rounded than mine ever was. And we agreed, you wouldn't take any more risks. You're not thinking of the family.
JT: Everything I do is for the family. It's decided.

    JT *leaves.*

ALICE: Why must you always be so miserable?
ELLEN MARY: I only want the best for you, Alice.
ALICE: How would you know what's best?
ELLEN MARY: I'm your mother.
ALICE: But you're trapped in the house all day with your injured leg. You don't even try!
ELLEN MARY: Is that what you think of me?
ALICE: Always waiting.
ELLEN MARY: One day, Alice, you will understand.
ALICE: We're going to have different lives, Ma.
ELLEN MARY: I'm sorry you think my life is so unpleasant.
ALICE: No! But I'm going to be out there, doing things. Like Da.
ELLEN MARY: You're not Da.
ALICE: Not yet. But I want to be.

SCENE 30

NARRATOR (4): With the twenties in full swing, there's a new energy in the air.
NARRATOR (2): Bitalli wins the Cup one year,
NARRATOR (3): And Backwood wins the next!
NARRATOR (2): Whispers of prohibition,
NARRATOR (1): And union strikes ripple through the streets!
NARRATOR (3): Miss Anderson is spotted everywhere: university lectures,
NARRATOR (4): Articles in *Women's Motoring*,
NARRATOR (3): Parties uptown—
RUTH: Alice!

> RUTH *corners* ALICE.

I've been trying to tell you for weeks. The regional tours have been more costly than rewarding. Do you need to provide them with a three-course meal?
ALICE: What is it, Snell?
RUTH: I've been trying to tell you for weeks. The regional tours have been more costly than rewarding. Do you need to provide them with a three-course meal?
ALICE: It's about customer satisfaction—setting ourselves apart—investment in future patronage.
RUTH: You have seventy-nine clients listed as 'doubtful debts'.
ALICE: Not all of them are lost!
RUTH: You've brought on eight girls. Not to mention the pay rise they've all been asking for.
ALICE: I told them I'm paying them as much as I can! They should be grateful. I know that Hilde Pickford's been stealing the soap!
RUTH: I think we need to slow down.
ALICE: If we slow down, we stop. We need to keep innovating.
RUTH: Do you really need the Overland Tourer?
ALICE: Of course I do! The American model has balloon tyres. To float over the road on cushions of air … streets ahead of the pneumatic tyre of the past.

RUTH: And the best oils? They're double the price and I doubt the customers would know any better.
ALICE: This is where you're wrong, Snell. It's what sets us apart. Which is why I put down a deposit on a Baby Austin.
RUTH: You bought an Austin?
ALICE: You buy a motorcar, Snell. You invest in an Austin.
RUTH: I don't understand.
ALICE: She's the smallest car ever built—it's like she's made for me.
RUTH: No, how did you pay for it?
ALICE: I made it work!
RUTH: But the books, Alice, we still—
ALICE: Someone owed me a favour. It'll put us on the map, Snell. Just have faith.

## SCENE 31

*Evening.* ALICE *is working in the garage, humming along to the radio.*

NARRATOR (3): Alice gets straight to work, exploring every corner of her beloved Austin.

*She hears the rumble of an engine.*

*She quickly turns off the radio and hides herself in the shadows.*

*A brick, suddenly, smashes through the window. Shards of glass are spilled out across the garage floor.*

*The screech of tyres.* ALICE *is left shaken.*

## SCENE 32

*The next morning.* ALICE *hasn't slept a wink.*

JESSIE: What on earth happened?
ALICE: A brick, straight through the window.
JESSIE: How medieval.
ALICE: I thought so too.
JESSIE: Do you know who it was?
ALICE: It could have been anyone.
JESSIE: Did they take anything?

ALICE: They didn't stay for tea!
JESSIE: You're ruffling feathers.
ALICE: I suppose that's a good thing.
JESSIE: Well. It is and isn't. Perhaps you should report it.
ALICE: It's not worth the trouble.
JESSIE: It's a brick this time, but what's next?
ALICE: [*referring to the book in* JESSIE's *hand*] A book of poetry? I loved the last one you gave me.
JESSIE: I'm surprised you had time to read it.
ALICE: Finished it in one night. Even committed some of them to memory.
JESSIE: Really?
ALICE: Yes.
JESSIE: Go on then.
ALICE: Now?
JESSIE: I'm listening.

   *Pause.*

ALICE: 'If in this shadowland of life thou hast
     Found one true heart to love them, hold it fast
     Love it again, give all to keep it thine
     For love like nothing in the world can last.'

   JESSIE *laughs.*

JESSIE: You're full of surprises, Alice! Well you'll love this book—it'll leave you longing to visit America.
ALICE: I do hope to travel the world some day, but I think everybody should know something about her own country first.
JESSIE: Carve your name into the map, perhaps.
ALICE: Yes—straight through the desert! 'A.A. was here.'
JESSIE: There's no doubt A.A. was here. Now, I have a proposition for you. The University has given me two tickets to *Pirates of Penzance* on Thursday …
ALICE: They're back in town, again?
JESSIE: Apparently, it's a hoot.
ALICE: Well, I am fond of Gilbert and Sullivan …

SCENE 33

NARRATOR (2): Weeks pass at Cotham Road. Alice doesn't sleep.
NARRATOR (1): But she never slept.

*The end of the working day.*

MAGGIE: Alice, are you coming?
ALICE: You go ahead.
MARIE: You promised!
ALICE: I said I'd think about it.
FLEURY: But the Pickle Sisters are playing!
ALICE: The who sisters?
MAGGIE: One night only! The Green Mill.
MARIE: Wait until you see their hats!
FLEURY: It is what we call, 'avant garde'.

ALICE *laughs, then winces and clutches her side.*

MAGGIE: Well—what do you say?
ALICE: I love parties as much as the next person, but the work is backed up and it has to get done.
FLEURY: I guess that's it then. We won't be seeing her!

*The* GARAGE GIRLS *exit with energy for their evening ahead.*

ALICE *continues her work on the motorcars, unaware of the arrival of* JT.

JT: Excuse me—
ALICE: Sorry, sir, we're closed—

*She looks up, her face brightens.*

JT: [*grinning*] I'd like to speak to the proprietor.
ALICE: Da! What are you doing here, I thought you were up in Albury?
JT: Can't a loving father pay a visit to his successful daughter?
ALICE: Sure you can! It's wonderful to see you!
JT: My, Alice, I'm sorry I haven't gotten back here sooner! This garage is as clean as a whistle.
ALICE: Look at this—came in yesterday, from Malvern—I thought of you as soon as it rolled in—that royal blue.

ALICE *and* JT *admire the motorcar.*

JT: It's grand, isn't it—what I wouldn't give to have one just like it—what does it need?

ALICE: [*excitedly*] Well: at first, I thought it was the coil, but then it bit me … So, I checked the spark-plug lead on the number-four cylinder—and it was dead! Turns out, it was a hairline crack that caused the misfire!

JT: No problem you couldn't solve!

ALICE: I don't know about that, Da.

JT: I mean it, Alice. Andersons always come out on top—eventually! Who else can say their daughter built a business from the ground up, brick-by-brick? Who sees the road ahead, as a golden opportunity to find what's waiting round the bend?

ALICE: Who do you think I got it from?

*They share a grin.* ALICE *claps her hands decisively.*

Let's make some tea!

JT: Love a cup of tea!

ALICE *makes motion towards the kettle.*

Now, let me tell you about an exciting prospect.

ALICE *stops.*

An opportunity we can't afford to miss.

ALICE: Not here for a social visit, then.

JT: Top secret, Alice! Insider trading and all. I'd love to tell you more, but I'd lose a finger.

ALICE: [*flatly*] How much.

JT: Not much at all Alice—you wouldn't even notice it's gone! The cream off the top of your coffee!

ALICE: How much?

JT: Fifty.

ALICE: Pounds or pence?

JT: Rapier wit, Alice!

ALICE: I can give you twenty pounds. Not that things are tight—they're not.

JT: You're my favourite daughter, Alice. I've always said it. Now, how about that tea?

*Small pause.*

ALICE: There's actually somewhere I need to be.

## SCENE 34

ALICE *tumbles into a swinging party.*

MAGGIE: You came!
ALICE: Of course!
FLEURY: Alice, people have been asking about you all night.
MARIE: They saw our uniforms and let us in for free!
ALICE: The work comes with benefits, Marie.
MAGGIE: Someone snuck a case of gin through the back door!
RUTH: Alice, the mayor is here—
ALICE: The mayor?! Where did you see him?
MAGGIE: Forget business for one night!
MARIE: Yes, Alice—come and dance!
ALICE: Alright!

*The* GARAGE GIRLS *shout with delight and dance.*

PARTY PERSON 1: Look—it's Alice!
PARTY PERSON 2: Alice Anderson! I've been dying to meet you!
ALICE: Why, it's a pleasure!
PARTY PERSON 1: I've got a picture of you in my room!
ALICE: Drop by and I'll sign it!
PARTY PERSON 4: You're an inspiration!
PARTY PERSON 3: What's it like?
ALICE: What's what like?
PARTY PERSON 1: What's next?
ALICE: Next?

ALICE *clutches her stomach.*

PARTY PERSON 2: Is it true you sleep where you work?
ALICE: Yes, but I—

*Suddenly the tone of the room shifts for* ALICE. *The music begins to morph and distort as if underwater. The partygoers are floating in a slowed-down state.* ALICE *begins to lose track of who is speaking to her.*

PARTY PERSON 3: In a garage FULL of girls!
ALICE: Not quite—
PARTY PERSON 2: Getting up to who-knows-what after the customers go home.
ALICE: That's not—
PARTY PERSON 4: It's the worst-kept secret in town …
ALICE: What secret?
PARTY PERSON 1: Degenerate.

*The world blurs.* ALICE *feels another sharp pain in her stomach.*

MECHANIC 2: We told you we'd be back.
FLEURY: Alice, Mr Henry's Buick is here.
ALICE: [*startled*] Already?
MECHANIC 2: We know who you are.
ALICE: Leave me alone.
PARTY PERSON 1: Aren't you a funny little fella—
MECHANIC 2: You ought to be ashamed.
MARIE: Another Once-Over!
ALICE: For who?
PARTY PERSON 1: Want to dance?
ALICE: No—
MECHANIC 2: It's a dangerous game.
FLEURY: Alice?
MECHANIC 2: Look at you.
MARIE: Alice, the Pickles are about to sing!
ALICE: I've got to go.
PARTY PERSON 1: No, come back.
ALICE: I've got to get out of here.
FLEURY: Are you alright?
ALICE: I've got to get out of here!

*ALICE shrieks in pain, clutching her stomach. A light hits her, time slows down momentarily. An idea strikes. She collapses.*

*Blackout.*

## SCENE 35

*Two weeks later. The* GARAGE GIRLS *are busy with their work.* ALICE *enters, surprising everyone.*

MARIE: Alice, shouldn't you be resting?
ALICE: It's only a ruptured appendix. It was a useless organ anyway.
RUTH: Alice, please! The nurses say you're the most overworked person they've seen since the war—
ALICE: How amusing—
MAGGIE: Are you sure you're up for it?
ALICE: I was going stir-crazy in that hospital bed.
FLEURY: It's a long way from here, Alice.
ALICE: I know! Which is why I'm doing it! After this, everyone will know our name.
MAGGIE: What are we going to do without you?
ALICE: You'll be fine! I've given Snell all the notes.
RUTH: It was quite comprehensive.
FLEURY: Alice, you must be joking. The Baby Austin is too small for this kind of trip.
MAGGIE: How are you going to fit everything in?
ALICE: I've removed the doors, for that very reason!
FLEURY: [*to* ALICE] That's absurd.
ALICE: It's a genius modification. I'll be able to fit in an extra gallon of water.
FLEURY: Does Jessie know about this?
ALICE: She's been to Africa and the Middle East. She's used to travelling rough.
MAGGIE: It won't be the same without you.
ALICE: It's only six weeks.
RUTH: We're going to miss you.
ALICE: I'll miss you too.

    *Beat.*

Don't forget to feed the cat.
MARIE: We've got a cat?

*SCENE 36*

NARRATOR (2): Outside the Lyceum Club: there's a flash of a camera!
NARRATOR (3): Champagne flutes are passed from hand to hand, as the crowd admires Alice's Baby Austin Seven.
ALICE: It's a three thousand, five hundred and fifty-eight-mile return journey and we're setting out in the smallest car ever built.
WOMAN 1: There's one main road from Adelaide to Alice Springs and it's a camel track. Will you stick to that?
ALICE: We'll be following our noses.
JESSIE: We're well-equipped!
WOMAN 2: What will you be taking?
ALICE: Sleeping bags, a shovel, an axe, four gallons of water—roped to the running boards. A shotgun for extra protection and sweets and tobacco to give to the people we meet.
WOMAN 3: You're travelling light!
WOMAN 2: You're a braver woman than I.
JESSIE: It'll certainly be a new experience.
WOMAN 1: What do you say to those who think anyone who takes a trip into the interior for pleasure must be … a lunatic?
ALICE: I say, getting accustomed to the conditions is half the spice of adventure!
WOMAN 2: Hear hear!
WOMAN 3: How will the garage cope without you?
ALICE: My loyal second-in-charge, Snell, is perfectly capable. We've been planning this journey for a month. The road is built for those that dare to travel. Thank you and see you on the other side.

> ALICE *and* JESSIE *wave, as the Lyceum Club members applaud with enthusiasm.*

*SCENE 37*

NARRATOR (3): Instead of taking the direct route inland, Alice and Jessie drive the unfinished and dangerous Great Ocean Road.
NARRATOR (1): Through Torquay, around to Lorne, up to Apollo Bay— they follow the majestic road curving into the rugged cliff.

NARRATOR (2): At the Eastern View tollgate, Alice pays two shillings sixpence as the driver. Jessie pays one shilling and sixpence as the passenger.
NARRATOR (3): They cross the border and continue west to Mount Gambier, surrounded by picturesque lakes and an extinct volcano.
NARRATOR (1): We catch up with them on the edge of the desert.

    ALICE *and* JESSIE *survey the landscape.*

JESSIE: See those scarlet peas in the distance?
ALICE: They look like bright parrots squatting on the roadside!
JESSIE: How spectacular.
ALICE: My sister Frankie would put this in perfect paint. [*Looking to the motorcar*] Baby's even faster than I imagined.
JESSIE: This looks like a fine spot to camp.
ALICE: Don't you want to see the caves, with the fossils of the giant wombats? We could get there before sundown if we keep going.
JESSIE: We don't need to beat a crowd! We can see them tomorrow.
ALICE: [*smiling*] Last I checked, I'm the driver. So unless you want to take the wheel, let's press on.
JESSIE: Alright.
ALICE: You'll love the fossils. I promise.

## SCENE 38

*The middle of a sunny day.* ALICE *has popped the bonnet of the Austin, working on the engine.*

ALICE: Pass me the wrench, would you?
JESSIE: How bad is it?
ALICE: Nothing I can't fix.
JESSIE: I don't doubt that. But the sun is beating down.
ALICE: Just a few more minutes.
JESSIE: We should find a nice spot to eat in the shade.
ALICE: I think there's an outpost up ahead.
JESSIE: Any requests for lunch?
ALICE: Surprise me.

    *They share a smile.*

SCENE 39

*They press on. One week later. Night.*
ALICE *stomps on the ground.*

JESSIE: What on earth are you doing?
ALICE: We don't want snakes for bedfellows.
JESSIE: Oh, Alice.
ALICE: Come on!

> JESSIE *joins* ALICE *as they both stomp for a moment, laughing. They plonk themselves down.*
>
> JESSIE *points to the star-lit sky.*

JESSIE: See there, in the crux constellation? The people of this land call it the Ginan. It's the smallest of the stars, yet look how brightly it shines.

> JESSIE *glances at* ALICE. ALICE *glances at* JESSIE, *then again at the sky.*

ALICE: Don't you just long to be up there, soaring through the stars?
JESSIE: I have travelled the world and yet I have never encountered such a hungry heart as yours!
ALICE: Why would I not want to suck the marrow out of life?
JESSIE: Of course, but—
ALICE: I want to know how it feels to dip my toes in the fairy pools of Skye. To walk the rainforests of South America! The motorcar is just the beginning. You know what they're saying about air travel … going to sleep in one place and waking up in another. It's otherworldly. It's nothing short of … magic.
JESSIE: Yet, I think that as you have your eyes on the horizon, you're missing what's right in front of you.
ALICE: And what is it that I'm missing that's right in front of me?
JESSIE: There's no-one here but us, Alice.

> JESSIE *and* ALICE *touch hands.*

SCENE 40

*Days have passed. The middle of the desert.*

JESSIE: There you are! I turned around for a moment and you were gone.
ALICE: I saw this remarkable wedge-tailed eagle flying overhead.
JESSIE: You scared me, disappearing like that.
ALICE: I was coming back.

SCENE 41

*A week later.* ALICE *and* JESSIE *have pulled over by the side of the dirt track. They gaze at the horizon.*

JESSIE: What are you thinking?
ALICE: I'm thinking … a fleet of motor homes. Tiny moving houses … crossing through the desert sand.

> JESSIE *watches on, silent.*

SCENE 42

*On the road.*

JESSIE: We're lost!
ALICE: Never admit to your passengers you don't know where you are.
JESSIE: I'm not just a passenger. Where are we? We should be near Coober Pedy.
ALICE: I took a detour.
JESSIE: We can't afford to take a detour. We're low on supplies. The water drum's nearly empty.
ALICE: I've marked it, I've counted the miles, we can do it. The Baby can do it.
JESSIE: Alice, this was not the plan.
ALICE: I thought you'd like the adventure.

## SCENE 43

*The middle of the night.*

JESSIE: Alice, what are you doing—
ALICE: Shh!
JESSIE: What is it?
ALICE: Shh!
JESSIE: What—

    ALICE *notices something.*

ALICE: Pass me the gun.
JESSIE: Alice—
ALICE: Pass me the gun!

    *The scream of a young girl is heard.*

FRANKIE: Ah! Alice—
ALICE: Frankie?

    ALICE *has fallen into a memory.*

What is it?
FRANKIE: The dog, her—her leg—
ALICE: What's wrong with her?

    JESSIE *looks around, confused.*

JESSIE: What are you talking about?
FRANKIE: The fence. She's trapped—I can't untangle her—
ALICE: Show me where she is.
JESSIE: Alice?

    ALICE *cocks the gun.*

FRANKIE: You can't shoot her!
ALICE: We don't have a choice.
JESSIE: Who are you talking to?
ALICE: I'm sorry. I'm so sorry.
FRANKIE: No! Please. We can save her.
ALICE: It's too late.
JESSIE: For what?

ALICE: Look away.

> ALICE *takes aim and shoots the dog. A loud bang. The moaning stops.* FRANKIE *disappears.*

JESSIE: Alice!

> ALICE *is snapped out of her reverie.*

What's going on?

> *A moment.*

ALICE: I thought I saw … nothing.

## SCENE 44

ALL LOCALS: Welcome to Alice Springs!
NARRATOR (3): A small gathering of enthusiastic locals and press have gathered around the pair.
LOCAL 2: How are you feeling?
ALICE: In need of a bath!
LOCAL 1: What do you say to your sponsors?
ALICE: Thank you for supporting us! Thanks to Butler Nicholson and Universal Oils, used solely throughout the trip! She's a trusty car. We were in good hands!
LOCAL 2: A trip not for the faint-hearted!
JESSIE: It was certainly a new experience in hardship.
ALICE: I never realised my life in the bush as a child has toughened me up.
LOCAL 3: Are you ready to tackle the return trip?
ALICE: We made it this far—we're proof that it's possible!

> *The crowd applauds.*

## SCENE 45

JESSIE *stands with a suitcase.*

ALICE: What are you doing?
JESSIE: I've packed my things and I've left you the maps.
ALICE: What do you mean?
JESSIE: I'm going home, Alice.

ALICE: Going home? Don't be ridiculous.
JESSIE: It's the first sane idea I've had this whole trip.
ALICE: We only just arrived.
JESSIE: I know.
ALICE: … How are you going to get home without me?
JESSIE: There's a train leaving this afternoon.
ALICE: What's the matter with you?
JESSIE: Me?! The last hundred miles you barely spoke a word.
ALICE: That's not true. I've been taking care of us.
JESSIE: Yes—and you're remarkably capable at taking care of us. But I didn't come here to get lost and bitten and to almost die in the desert.
ALICE: What did you expect?
JESSIE: Not this.
ALICE: We're making history. We've set a record. Don't you understand?
JESSIE: Is that all this was to you?
ALICE: What else was it meant to be?
JESSIE: Why did you ask me to come with you?
ALICE: Because … you said you wanted to come.
JESSIE: That's not why you asked me. You asked me because you need me. I know what you're afraid of.
ALICE: I'm not afraid of anything.
JESSIE: Yes, you are.
ALICE: You think I couldn't have done this, alone?
JESSIE: No. You couldn't! I see you, Alice, and I know you see me.
ALICE: Stop it—
JESSIE: There's too much between us now. Together, alone, in the middle of the desert.
ALICE: Don't—
JESSIE: Why else would you bring me out here? I know how hard it can be for people like us—
ALICE: There is no 'us'. I'm here for one reason and it has nothing to do with you. I know I was born now, to make something of this time, this moment—it's not a mistake I'm here! It's not a mistake that I am who I am. And I'm not going to stop for anyone.

*A small pause.*

JESSIE: You're right. And I'm just slowing you down.

    JESSIE *exits*.

ALICE: Jessie, wait … Jessie? Jessie!

    ALICE *looks around in fear. She is suddenly alone.*

## SCENE: 46

*In the terrifying emptiness of the desert,* ALICE *drops to her knees and prays.*

ALICE: Give me strength: In this, my time of need,
    Help me hold firm in my faith.
    Help me hold firm in my faith.
    Help me hold firm in my—

AMELIA: You are here!

    *A figure emerges from the horizon. She resembles* AMELIA EARHART. *Is it a mirage?*

ALICE: Ah! I thought I was alone!

    ALICE *is startled.*

AMELIA: You're not alone.

ALICE: It's so empty. I don't know which way to turn.

AMELIA: The choices are endless. They can make you mad. Who are we?

ALICE: Who are we? Who are we … ?

AMELIA: Darlin', if I had a dime for every time I'd doubted myself.

ALICE: Who says I'm doubting?

AMELIA: Everyone has oceans to fly, if they have the heart to do it. You know that.

ALICE: Maybe I am afraid.

AMELIA: What do dreams know of boundaries? We want to do it because we want to do it. Why not aim for the sky?!

ALICE: Will it be enough?

AMELIA: We're mavericks, you and I.

ALICE: Some people were meant to dream beyond what is possible.

AMELIA: Is it reckless? Maybe. Is it hard? Definitely.

ALICE: [*with desperation*] Then what do I do?

AMELIA: Life is short. [*To herself, walking away*] I'm thinking of a magnificent twin motor, all-metal, perfectly equipped for long-distance flights …

   *A telephone rings in the distance.*

ALICE: Tell me what to do!

AMELIA: San Francisco to Honolulu—England to Australia, Australia to—see you on the other side …

   AMELIA *disappears.*

   *The ringing stops.* ELLEN MARY *emerges.*

ELLEN MARY: Alice?

ALICE: Oh, Mother! It's you.

ELLEN MARY: Who else would it be? Where are you, Alice?

   ALICE *looks around.*

ALICE: Oodnadatta, I think.

ELLEN MARY: Oodnadatta.

ALICE: It's wonderful to hear the sound of home.

ELLEN MARY: Oh, Alice, that's awfully sentimental of you.

ALICE: Can't a daughter be awfully sentimental with her dear mother?

ELLEN MARY: Well I'm sure she can, on occasion. When are you coming home?

ALICE: Yes. Yes I'm coming home. I just need to find the way.

ELLEN MARY: You've always known the way, Alice.

ALICE: Have I?

ELLEN MARY: You just need to make a choice.

ALICE: Mother, I have to go.

   *She looks up to the sky.*

The rain is about to crack open the desert.

ELLEN MARY: Rain in the desert—who would hear of such a thing?

ALICE: It's a land of extremes, Mother. Much like myself.

   ELLEN MARY *disappears.* ALICE *looks up at the sky.*

SCENE 47

NARRATOR (2): On the outskirts of Oodnadatta, a local man surveys the Baby Austin.
OODNADATTA MAN: Are you sure? One hundred pounds.
ALICE: I'm sure.
OODNADATTA MAN: What's wrong with it?
ALICE: Nothing. She's perfect. She can handle anything that's thrown at her. She's loyal, smooth and feisty—when she needs to be.
OODNADATTA MAN: Aren't you that young girl I've read about in the papers? Why, I've seen ya picture! You're on the grand tour through the Never-Never. Surely you'll want to flaunt it when you're back in Melbourne?
ALICE: No. She did what she set out to do. And now we're finished.
OODNADATTA MAN: I thought you'd be taller.
ALICE: Excuse me?
OODNADATTA MAN: Taller, I thought you'd be taller, reading about your travels, everything you've done!
ALICE: People aren't often what you expect.

SCENE 48

*The garage. The* GARAGE GIRLS *are hard at work. The telephone rings relentlessly.*

MARIE: Snell, it's the Jessops! They've phoned three times already—
RUTH: We'll have it done by two!
MARIE: But little Nancy's stranded out in Nar Nar Goon!
MAGGIE: Snell, it's stuck, it's stuck!
RUTH: Put your back into it, Dodd!
MARIE: What's that steam?
FLEURY: It's not steam, it's smoke!
MAGGIE: This Adler was all over the road like a drunk duck—
FLEURY: You still know nothing about front-axle assemblies—
RUTH: I know it's been a hard week.
MAGGIE: Well, what do I do?

    ALICE *enters the garage, unaware to all.*

RUTH: Have you done a / wheelbase check?
ALICE: Wheelbase check?

    ALICE *drops her suitcases.*

RUTH: Alice!
FLEURY: Welcome home, Alice!
MAGGIE: We didn't expect you until tomorrow!
ALICE: I couldn't wait a moment longer.
MARIE: Thank God you're back!
ALICE: I'm glad to see the place is still standing—I knew you could do it, Ruth!
RUTH: Who's Ruth?

    RUTH *smiles.*

ALICE: My dear Snell, thank you.
FLEURY: My, you're suntanned, Alice!
ALICE: Sunburnt!
MAGGIE: We've been up to our ears—
MARIE: Thank God you're back!
FLEURY: We want to hear all about your travels—
RUTH: We kept up with all your telegrams.
MAGGIE: Did you think about us?
ALICE: Every day. You wouldn't believe the colours out there. Red sands, patches of royal purple peas that spread over the ground like a thick carpet.
MARIE: What were the people like?
ALICE: Just like us! They don't follow extreme fashions, but they look jolly nice. Nearly all the women I saw had shingled hair!
MARIE: Shingled hair!
RUTH: We've got something to show you. Arrived yesterday!
FLEURY: Couldn't believe they wanted to house it here!
MAGGIE: It's the most elegant car I've ever seen.

    RUTH *walks* ALICE *over to show her the vehicle.*

RUTH: A Rolls-Royce Twenty! Six-cyclinder—
FLEURY: Silk velvet upholstery—
MAGGIE: And look! There's an ivory speaking tube—for the passengers to give us directions!
MARIE: Look at the built-in vases! For flowers! Can you believe it?

RUTH: [*beaming*] What do you think?

*The* GARAGE GIRLS *wait in anticipation for* ALICE*'s reaction.*

*A small pause.*

ALICE: It's a beauty.
FLEURY: It's more than a beauty, Alice.
MAGGIE: Don't you want to take a peek at the engine?
ALICE: I trust one of you will do a fine job.

*Small pause.*

RUTH: We thought you'd be over the moon.
ALICE: I am—but I've been thinking: no-one believed us when we started—automobiles, our garage … and now, Australia is on the eve of an aviation boom!
RUTH: Alice—what are you talking about?
ALICE: Aeroplanes! We could fly Melbourne to the outback, as quickly as a motor tour from Kew to the Peninsula!

ALICE *laughs.*

MAGGIE: She's got a touch of the sun.
ALICE: Everyone has oceans to fly, if they have the heart to do it.
FLEURY: But you don't know how to fly.
ALICE: Not yet! My first stop off the train this morning was to the aviation academy. I've applied for my pilot's licence. Announcing 'Miss Anderson's Flying School'.
RUTH: You're leaving Cotham Road?
ALICE: Not leaving.
MAGGIE: What about us?
ALICE: You're coming with me.
FLEURY: Who will run the garage?
ALICE: I will. We can do both!
MARIE: You just got here.
ALICE: Ideas don't stop. You can't stop ideas!
MAGGIE: But what about—
ALICE: It's the future, girls, the future, and I want you all to be a part of it!

*The* GARAGE GIRLS *look to one another.*

SCENE 49

*The garage. Night.*
*The sound of a gunshot.*
*Sirens wail.*

SCENE 50

*The garage. The next morning.*

RUTH: The detective's coming.
MARIE: Why?
RUTH: To ask us questions: where we were, what we were doing—
MARIE: But it was an accident.
RUTH: A horrible accident.
MARIE: She was cleaning it.
RUTH: Was she?
MARIE: I called the doctor …
RUTH: You were here?
MARIE: She was still breathing …
RUTH: What did you do?
MARIE: I loosened her tie …

    MAGGIE *enters.*

MAGGIE: It's not possible! It's just not possible.
MARIE: The detective's coming.
MAGGIE: How could this have happened?
RUTH: She ruffled feathers.
MAGGIE: No-one would go that far.
RUTH: Wouldn't they?
MARIE: The back door was open.
MAGGIE: Would she?
RUTH: What are you saying?
MAGGIE: She knew how to handle a gun.
RUTH: She wouldn't. She would never. She wouldn't do that to herself.

    FLEURY *enters.*

FLEURY: What's going on?

> *Beat.*

MAGGIE: Alice is dead.

## SCENE 51

NARRATOR (1): A memory. Alice, Claire, Frankie, JT and Ellen Mary stand outside Miss Cattach's wooden shed at Cotham Road, Kew.
ALICE: Well, what do you think?
JT: Alice, where did you get the money for the bricks?
ALICE: Never mind where I got the money. What do you think?
FRANKIE: It's beautiful.
CLAIRE: You'll need some flowers for the sill.
ALICE: You'll paint my business cards, won't you, Frankie?
FRANKIE: Of course I will.
ALICE: What do you think, Mother?
ELLEN MARY: There's no-one quite like you, Alice.
ALICE: I've got a good feeling about this.

## SCENE 52

*The* GARAGE GIRLS *speak to the audience.*

RUTH: Some of us stayed friends.
MAGGIE: Some of us lost touch.
FLEURY: Nothing like those days at Cotham Road, Kew.
MAGGIE: Some of us kept it going—
RUTH: For as long as we could.
FLEURY: Before the doors closed for the very last time.
MARIE: There's been nothing like it before or since.
MAGGIE: But that spark—
FLEURY: That spark she lit—
MARIE: How could we forget?
RUTH: The look on everyone's faces—
FLEURY: When they stepped through the door—
MAGGIE: And saw that we were all girls.

> *The* GARAGE GIRLS *exit.*

*EPILOGUE*

NARRATOR (4): Light beams from the headlights of a motorcar. This is Alice. Alice Anderson.

 *The* NARRATOR *melts away, leaving only* ALICE.

ALICE: 'For me the hills—no winding valley ways
    Hemming me in and sheltering my days;
    For me the effort, the vast, far flung goal,
    Great draughts of beauty for my thirsting soul.
    From far above, the mists that drift below
    Drown the soft azure beauty sin and woe;
    And oh the joy of conquest, looking back to say:
    "My feet are bruised, but I have climbed today!"'

THE END

www.ingramcontent.com/pod-product-compliance
Lightning Source LLC
Chambersburg PA
CBHW050026090426
42734CB00021B/3437